GARDEN
WISDOM

GARDEN WISDOM

Copyright © Summersdale Publishers Ltd, 2013

Images and icons © Shutterstock

Summersdale Publishers Ltd
46 West Street
Chichester
West Sussex
PO19 1RP
UK

www.summersdale.com

Printed and bound in China

ISBN: 978-1-84953-386-7

Substantial discounts on bulk quantities of Summersdale books are available to corporations, professional associations and other organisations. For details contact Nicky Douglas by telephone: +44 (0) 1243 756902, fax: +44 (0) 1243 786300 or email: nicky@summersdale.com.

GARDEN
WISDOM

Felicity Hart

Contents

Introduction

When it comes to the garden, a little bit of wisdom can go a long way. Within these pages you will find helpful tips, snippets of intriguing garden lore and delightful quotations covering the most essential aspects of the art of horticulture, from planning your plants to keeping everything healthy and happy. Each chapter provides an array of pithy pointers, and for those who would like to cultivate their garden wisdom a little more there is a Further Reading section which gives the details of more in-depth resources.

So what are you waiting for? Have your gardening gloves at the ready while you read on and let your enthusiasm blossom!

Best Laid Plans

Size and Shape

Whether creating a new garden or reimagining an existing one, there are a number of key assessments to be made. Firstly, evaluate the size and shape of your plot. You should look to accommodate all of your plants comfortably, with enough room for everything to grow unhindered – trees especially demand a lot of room! Also, consider how your features (if you're planning to install any) will fit in once your garden is established, ensuring they won't be swamped or damaged as your plants grow.

The garden must first be
prepared in the soul, or
else it will not flourish.

English proverb

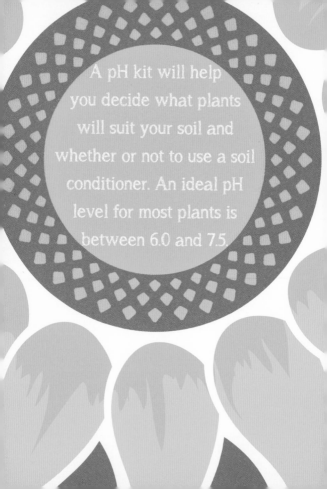

A pH kit will help you decide what plants will suit your soil and whether or not to use a soil conditioner. An ideal pH level for most plants is between 6.0 and 7.5.

Light

Consider the direction your garden faces – this will affect the amount of sun the garden receives and therefore determine what kind of plants will thrive, as well as their position on the plot. Find out which way your garden faces by using a compass or a map – a south-facing garden will receive light all day, whereas a north-facing garden will struggle to receive any. East-facing and west-facing gardens will get a mix of sun and shade throughout the day.

Soil

Most plants will benefit from soil that drains well. To determine your garden's drainage properties, dig a small hole about 1 foot deep; fill the hole with water and allow it to drain completely. Next, fill the hole again and immediately measure the depth of the water. Return 15 minutes later and take another measurement. Multiply this measurement by four to calculate the drainage per hour. Between 1 and 6 inches per hour is workable, though somewhere near the middle of this scale is best. Use your findings to determine how you could develop your garden.

Garden Lore

Parsley will only grow
outside the home of
an honest man or
a strong woman.

Indigenous Plants

To help you decide what to plant, take a look at the existing vegetation in your plot or, if you're working with a clean slate, in a garden nearby. If you like the look of something growing in a nearby garden, why not pay the owner a visit and ask for some clippings or seeds from flower heads, or take stem cuttings from woody shrubs? The precise method for achieving best results will depend on the variety of plant, however it may help to dip your stems in rooting powder and plant in moist soil in a pot out of direct sunlight.

Tooling Up

Quality, Not Quantity

Before going out and buying every shiny new tool you see, take some time to consider what, realistically, you will need for the job at hand. Seek out places where you might find pre-owned tools – car boot sales, agricultural fairs and online auction sites. If you're buying new, talk to someone at your local garden centre to get an idea of reliable manufacturers and be sure to handle each tool before you buy it – there's no point in spending money on something that's uncomfortable to use!

Other people's tools
only work in other
people's gardens.

Arthur Bloch

Use antibacterial wipes when cleaning your pruners to ensure they don't pick up and spread any diseases or bacteria.

Good Working Order

Once you've parted with your hard-earned cash for some quality tools, it is advisable to take a little time to keep them in good working order. Help prevent rust by wiping the metal portions of your tools down with an oily rag after each use, and be sure to hang tools up, away from the ground, if you're stowing them in your shed or garage. Running a file over any cutting edges can help keep them sharp – just be sure to use protective eyewear and gloves.

Keeping Tabs

A great way to organise your plants and seedlings is to paint the collars of their pots with stripes of paint, designating a colour for each variety. Alternatively, why not use a set of flat, smooth stones, marked with permanent ink, which can be placed in your pots or flower beds as more natural-looking markers. And if you and your family are keen on ice lollies, keep the sticks, as they too can be used to label your plants.

Garden Lore

Never carry a hoe into
the house or bad luck is
sure to follow.

Little Extras

There are dozens of useful little extras that can make your gardening experience more successful. A ball of weatherproof twine will come in handy for all sorts of jobs, from tying plants to hanging bird feeders – make it easier to use by mounting it on a nail in the shed. Netting can be used both for protecting plants from pests (fine-gauge) to trellising (heavy-gauge), as well as for ponds. For the colder months, synthetic fleece is a great way to protect your plants against the elements.

Recycling
in the
Garden

Recycle and Reuse

Even when you think you've got yourself fully kitted out to manage and maintain your garden, there is bound to be something else you find you need at some point. However, you need not go rushing to the garden centre – you may have the perfect tool or aid for the job sitting in your home! Take a minute to consider if there's anything lying around the house that could perform the function of the tool you're after. For example, old tights make great plant ties, and cardboard toilet-roll tubes are ideal pots for seedlings.

Use it up, wear it out,
make it do or do
without.

Proverb

Use a water butt connected to a drainpipe to catch rainwater for hydrating your plants – fit a secure lid to stop debris getting inside and turning the water stagnant.

Odds and Sods

There are plenty of ways you can reuse everyday household items to help make gardening that little bit more cost-effective. For example, an old screwdriver will do the job of a dibber just as efficiently, and a traditional-style potato peeler can be great for uprooting small weeds. If you're short of a kneeling pad, fill an old hot-water bottle with polystyrene chips or other soft packing material. Unwanted CDs and DVDs can be dangled from a line to act as bird-scarers on a veg patch, but be wary of leaving them out too long as they may go brittle and break up in the sun.

Waste Not, Want Not

Give a second life to your rubbish by using it in your garden. Cut the tops off plastic drinks bottles to make mini cloches for protecting seedlings from bad weather and slugs. Empty plastic milk bottles make great water feeders – simply pierce them at the bottom, bury them in your flower bed (with the open top visible) and fill with water as and when is needed. Bubble wrap can function as a pot warmer, instead of fleece, but be aware that it's not breathable.

Garden Lore

A sliced onion pressed
onto an insect bite relieves
the itch and prevents
swelling.

Everything, Including the Kitchen Sink

Even the most unlikely items can be put to some use in the garden. Quirky planters can be created from anything from old wellies to unwanted bathtubs – as well as kitchen sinks.

To make your planter:

- Line the inside with plastic (reusing old shopping bags is a good idea)
- Ensure your planter has a hole (or holes) for drainage – make your own if necessary
- Place a layer of stones or broken pots at the bottom and fill with compost
- Plant your seeds or young plants, add another layer of soil, and water

Earthy
Goodness

Checking your Soil Type

As well as assessing the pH level of your soil, it's useful to have an idea of its basic make-up. If you turn your soil and you find stones littered throughout, it's likely that you have chalky soil – this will be highly alkaline and will dry out quickly. Clay soil is easily identified by its dense consistency – it will need a lot of loosening for adequate aeration. Conversely, sandy soil, being fine, will lose moisture quickly and be lacking in healthy organic matter. Loam soil, with a mix of sand, silt and clay, is ideal.

To forget how to dig the
earth and tend the soil
is to forget ourselves.

Mahatma Gandhi

Things to
leave out of your compost
include: cooked food, meat scraps,
droppings, perennial weed roots,
diseased plant material,
thick woody stems
and prickly
leaves.

Compost

One of the simplest ways to improve your soil, whichever type it may be, is to add organic matter in the form of compost. This will improve soil structure – helping sandy soil retain moisture and breaking down clumpy clay soil – as well as introducing microorganisms that create plant-available nutrients. The ideal compost heap will be no smaller than 1 cubic metre, be around 50 per cent soft green material (grass trimmings, weeds, fruit and veg scraps, etc.) and 50 per cent brown woody material (wood chips, dead leaves, card, etc.), and be constructed in layers.

Conditioning your Soil

You needn't stop at compost if you're keen to improve the condition of your soil. Here's a table showing a number of other popular conditioners and their effects:

Conditioner	Effects
Composted bark	Improves aeration and drainage in clay soils.
Manure	Enriches nutrients and encourages worms giving better aeration.
Lime	Neutralises acidity in sandy soils.

Garden Lore

An old farmer's proverb
goes: if you till the soil in
April showers, you will
have neither fruit
nor flowers.

pH Proper

As well as conditioning your soil, it's best to select plants that will thrive in its existing state. Plants like heather, witch hazel, camellias and rhododendrons will fare well in acidic soils. For alkaline soils, things like lilac, Madonna lily, delphiniums, poppies and mock orange will do well.

Lawn Talk

Turf v. Seed

If you're looking to establish a lawn on a new plot, you may want to consider whether or not to sow your lawn or simply lay turf. Sowing your lawn may provide you with more options in terms of what grass you grow – however, it is by no means instant, and seeds are prone to being eaten by birds or washed away. Turf, on the other hand, comes ready-made, but can be costly and limits your choice of grass type. The most important thing to remember, whichever route you plump for, is to make sure you water the patch thoroughly for the first few weeks to allow for adequate germination and rooting.

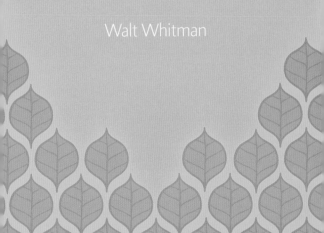

I believe a leaf of
grass is no less than
the journey-work
of the stars.

Walt Whitman

Refrigerate grass seeds for a couple of days before sowing to encourage more vigorous growth.

Repairs

A common problem for many gardeners is dealing with bare patches on their lawn, which are best repaired during spring or autumn. If using turf, cut out the offending patch as a square, lift carefully, lightly turn the soil underneath and lay the new turf in its place and water in. If using seeds, follow the same process to prepare the new patch, then add a layer of compost, scatter your seeds, cover with another layer of compost and water in.

Mowing

The mowing year begins in March, when the grass begins to grow with vigour, and ends in October, when growth stops. Aim to mow the lawn once a week in spring and autumn, but you may need to mow twice a week in the height of summer. Mow only when the grass is dry – mowing wet grass can lead to roots being stripped out and moss growing in its place.

Garden Lore

According to American folklore, if a dog is seen to eat grass it will almost certainly rain by nightfall.

Further Lawn Care

Give your lawn a makeover in the spring by first raking over the area and then pricking the soil with a pitchfork. Get some sand and sprinkle it all over the lawn, then brush the sand into the holes with a broom. When watering your lawn during dry spells, be aware that you may need to water it as much as twice a week in the height of summer. Fallen autumn leaves may look beautiful, but be sure to rake them off the lawn to prevent the grass from yellowing underneath.

Flower Power

Decisions, Decisions

If you're unsure as to what flowers to introduce into a new garden, don't be afraid to seek advice from your local nursery. One way to ensure that a given plant is hardy enough for your garden is to look out for the Royal Horticultural Society Award of Garden Merit, which means the plant has been tested and approved by the RHS. And of course, it's better to use plants in your garden that are native to your area or that have been imported from areas with similar climates and soil.

Earth laughs
in flowers.

Ralph Waldo Emerson

An arrangement of blue and orange flowers can have a soothing effect on nerves and anxiety.

Firm Favourites

Everyone has their favourites when it comes to flowers, however there are some varieties which will always be popular. Daffodils are a delightful harbinger of spring – choose smaller varieties like narcissus to ensure they don't get blown over in bad weather. Crocuses like the shade, so plant them around the base of a tree or hedge, whereas tulips are sun-lovers, so put them in a sunny spot with good drainage.

The Gift of Flowers

When giving flowers, take a moment to consider the connotations; here are a few of the most popular varieties and their meanings:

Daffodil – a desire to be loved
Fresia – friendship
Hyacinth – an appeal for forgiveness
Primrose – I can't live without you
Sunflower – homage and devotion
Sweet william – finesse and perfection

Garden Lore

A British tradition instructs
that red and white flowers
should not be given to
someone in hospital,
as these two colours
together signify blood
and bandages.

Leafy Allies

Planting a few foxgloves in the garden will stimulate growth in surrounding plants and help to fend off diseases. Another ally can be found in the humble stinging nettle – if you're weeding these out, consider leaving a few of them intact, as they will also stimulate growth and attract butterflies. Marigolds are excellent bedfellows for beans, carrots and potatoes as they release nitrogen into the soil.

Potting

Going Potty

One main point to consider when buying pots, aside from the essential questions of drainage and adequate size, is how well the pot's material will suit the plant that's going to be living in it. Traditional terracotta pots are pleasing to the eye but are porous and will allow soil to dry out quickly, and will sometimes crack after a heavy frost or snowfall. Heavier pots, made of wood, concrete or metal, are great for stabilising tall plants, while synthetic pots (plastic, etc.) conserve moisture and can easily be slipped into a more decorative container.

A flower is
an educated weed.

Luther Burbank

Keep snails away from potted plants by smearing Vaseline around the edge of the pot every couple of weeks.

Humidity

Placing your potted plants in close proximity to one another will mean that they will all benefit from the increased humidity this will create. However, be aware not to place them so close that their leaves are obstructed, as this will restrict their growth. If high humidity is a factor for your indoor potted plants, such as orchids, bromeliads and other more exotic plants, try placing them together on a tray of damp gravel.

Deadheading

Deadheading is essential for both indoor and outdoor potted plants. Pinch or cut off faded blooms to encourage further growth, making sure that the top part of the dead flower's stem comes off with it. This means the decaying stem won't affect any other healthy parts of the plant. If your plant has fine stems and very small flowers, it may benefit from an overall shearing, rather than a head-by-head tidy up. Always dispose of deadheads, rather than leave them in the pot.

Garden Lore

Plant hawthorn trees as
a hedgerow to keep
out bad luck and
mischievous spirits.

Holiday Maintenance

If you're planning to leave your potted plants unattended for a week or two, there are a number of things you can do to ensure they're still healthy upon your return. As a general rule for house plants, water them well and move them to an area of shade. For small plants, try placing them together in the bath, lined with an old damp towel. For thirstier plants, try filling a jug with water and placing a cotton rope from the jug to the pot – the rope will act as a wick, taking water to the plant slowly and steadily over time.

Fruits
of Your
Labours

Getting Fruity

Growing your own fruit can be very rewarding, not least because it is so versatile when it comes to turning it into food! If you're considering planting a fruiting tree, remember to think about how much room it will need so that it has enough space to flourish. Establish whether or not it's self-fertilising or if it will need to be paired with another tree. Self-fertile trees suited for the UK include 'Queen Cox' apples and 'Brown Turkey' figs. If trees sound heavy-going, why not grow some berry plants? Strawberries can be grown in pots, borders or hanging baskets.

In an orchard there should be enough to eat, enough to lay up, enough to be stolen and enough to rot on the ground.

James Boswell

If you find yourself forgetting to use your fresh herbs, why not pick them and dry them out? Store them in an airtight jar in a cool, dark place and they will last for up to two years.

Vegging Out

As with fruit plants, you needn't have an allotment to enjoy some home-grown produce. Plenty of veg can be grown in pots, such as bell peppers, chilli peppers, aubergines and tomatoes. Onions are a staple in countless dishes and, what's more, they are incredibly easy to grow – plant your baby onions (sets, as they are known) in spring, to harvest in late summer/ once the leaves have turned brown. If planting vegetables from seeds, as a general rule the larger the vegetable seed the deeper it should be sown – for carrots, half an inch, and for beans, 2 inches.

Simple Salads

All kinds of salads can be grown indoors on a windowsill, away from the elements, meaning that you're guaranteed a tasty treat without putting in lots of effort – and they'll keep growing back! A good tip to help your newly planted seeds on their way is to place a layer of cling film over your tray or pot – this will help keep the moisture in while they germinate. Once seedlings start to appear, remove the film. As soon as your salad leaves are around 3 inches tall you can start cutting.

Garden Lore

Never plant the same
herb in the same spot
twice or the second will
wither and fail.

Herbalicious

Many supermarkets stock ready-to-go herb pots, which can be ideal for the kitchen. However, it's easy to treat them like any other consumable and forget to look after them. For a more lasting and eco-friendly option, plant herbs in your garden instead. Grey-leafed herbs, such as rosemary and mint, are ideal for a sunny garden as they are drought resistant and will thrive without any special attention – however, you may want to plant them in pots and then sink them into the soil, to restrict their rampant growth.

Protecting
Your Plot

Beneficial Plants

If you have a vegetable patch, planting coreopsis, feverfew and sweet alyssum in the vegetable bed will attract beneficial insects that will happily munch away on pests such as aphids and whiteflies. Lavender is not only sweet-smelling but will also deter slugs, snails and aphids, and chives grown amongst rose bushes will help repel ants.

A thorn defends the rose, harming only those who would steal the blossom.

Chinese proverb

Red spider mites cause leaf discolouration: remove them by watering the affected plants daily with cold water.

Insect Pests

An eco-friendly way of getting on top of an aphid problem is to try to encourage more ladybirds into your garden – to accomplish this, why not try a 'Grow Your Own Ladybird Kit'? When your slug problem gets out of hand, fill a plastic tub or cup with (fresh) beer and place it on top of the soil near to the affected plant(s) to see off the slimy blighters. Fed up with earwigs in your dahlias? Fill a flowerpot with crumpled-up tissue and place upside down on a stick to tempt the little critters away to a new home.

Weather Protection

Aside from planting sensibly, there are a number of measures you can take to protect your plants in autumn and winter. Spraying them with cold water in the evening will actually help prevent frost damage, as the process of evaporation will generate heat. Another way of creating warmth to fend off frosts is to wrap the top-growth of susceptible shrubs like magnolias with horticultural fleece. Avoid walking on frozen or snow-covered lawns as this will cause unsightly marks once thawed.

Garden Lore

In ancient Greece, farmers believed that the best way to rid their crops of a mouse infestation was to write them a letter suggesting they find somewhere else to live!

Moles, Mice and Other Menaces

If you're plagued by a meddlesome mole, try sticking empty bottles upright, with their caps removed, in some of its hills – the sound of the wind blowing over the tops will help scare it away. Cats can be distracted from getting in amongst your delicate flowers with a clump of strategically placed cat mint, while regular mint, spread around the borders of your garden, will deter mice – that is, if the cat doesn't get to them first!

Weeding

The Good, the Bad and the Ugly

Weeds are almost always unsightly, but not all of them are useless. Clover is good for the lawn as it boosts the nitrogen in the soil and can be mown. Bindweed is deceptively pretty but bad news, as it will strangle plants and shrubs in borders. As an alternative to weed killer, try training it to grow up a bamboo cane placed close to the weed in spring. Dandelions are deep-rooted perennial weeds, so be sure to dig down far enough when cutting them out.

What is a weed?
A plant whose virtues
have not yet been
discovered.

Ralph Waldo Emerson

Pull when wet;
hoe when dry.

Eco-Friendly Control

As a first step to tackling persistent weeds, you may want to try a home-made weedkiller. Mix two parts boiling water with one part malt vinegar and decant into a spray bottle – this method will also work with salt, though be sure you only use this if you're not going to attempt to grow anything else in the spot you're treating (the salt will sterilise the soil). Use in dry, sunny conditions where possible.

Chemical Remedies

If you feel you need to resort to a chemical weed killer, aim to use a selective agent over a non-selective one. If applying to your lawn, avoid cutting the grass for at least a week and don't put the treated cuttings in your compost pile. Always read up on the product you're considering using and follow the instructions of use carefully.

Garden Lore

One year's seeding is
seven years' weeding.

If You Can't Beat Them, Eat Them

If your efforts to rid your garden of weeds are not paying off, then all is not lost – the right kind of weeds can be prepared for eating! Chickweed, clover, daisy flowers and leaves and dandelions can all be mixed in with salads to add some new and interesting flavours. Nettles can be used as a substitute for spinach and of course to make a tasty, fresh soup. Why not try making some dandelion flower vinegar? Simply add the flower heads to a jam jar full of cider vinegar and leave for around six weeks before using – delicious used in salad dressings!

Wildlife Sanctuary

Natural Habitats

One of the greatest pleasures of a garden, aside from the plant life itself, is the wildlife that it might attract. If you're keen to animate your garden with more birds, bees and butterflies, consider choosing plants that will provide a food source or a home for them – hedgerows and berry-producing shrubs provide food and shelter for birds and insects alike, nectar-rich flowers like asters and chrysanthemums will attract bees and butterflies, and cow parsley will attract hoverflies and lacewings.

Nothing exists for itself alone, but only in relation to other forms of life.

Charles Darwin

Encourage bats to feed in
your garden by growing
night-blooming flowers such
as moonflower and yucca.

Simple Additions

Birdfeeders are an easy way to attract more feathered visitors to your garden and are especially welcome in the winter when food may be scarce. Aim to buy a feeder with a squirrel guard, so the contents are received by the birds as intended. A log pile, left to break down over time, is a perfect home for many insects including stag beetle larvae, and a rock pile or rockery, with a number of empty spaces incorporated into the arrangement, will provide shelter for slug-eating frogs.

Tip-Top Trees

If you're looking to make more considerable additions to your garden, planting a few bird-friendly trees is a good place to start. Unless you have a vast expanse of garden, you may want to consider planting a medium-sized tree such as silver birch, hazel or beech, which all provide food for birds (and for insects, which birds will feed on). Fruit trees like crab apple and cherry will provide juicy offerings and dense evergreen and deciduous bushes are great for birds that need shelter.

Garden Lore

Old wives believe that
you will have good luck all
year if the first butterfly
you see is white.

Water Feature

A pond is perhaps the most diverse way of introducing new creatures into your garden – it can create homes for a host of insects and amphibians. If you plan to keep fish, however, be aware that they may be inclined to eat any frog spawn that's in the pond. Birds, including ducks, may visit to bathe or drink. Ensure that your pond has shallow and deep areas, along with sloping sides to make it easier for creatures to climb in and out.

Branching
Out

Size Matters

Before going out and buying trees for your garden, be sure to look into their growth rate. Leave enough space between each tree (and any other potential obstacle, natural or otherwise) to ensure that there's enough water and sunlight to go around. Also, be aware that trees will develop extensive, fast-growing root systems (poplar and willow are two examples) which may lead to subsidence if planted near to houses – take this into account, especially if your garden is in close proximity to your neighbour's.

I frequently tramped eight or ten miles through the deepest snow to keep an appointment with a beech tree or a yellow birch...

Henry David Thoreau

Use a
stem guard to
protect your saplings
from foraging animals.

iming is Everything

The ideal time to plant out shrubs is in the autumn, when the mix of sun and rain will provide the ideal conditions for roots to establish themselves before the winter. Once your trees have been in your garden long enough to need pruning, set about the task in later winter before any signs of new growth appear. Cut off damaged limbs and wayward branches.

Location, Location

If you live close to a road or a more urban area where your trees are likely to encounter a considerable amount of air pollution, consider planting more tolerant trees. These could include:

- maple
- horse chestnut
- alder
- silver birch
- poplar

Garden Lore

According to an ancient British tradition, the secret to eternal youth is to carry an acorn about your person, as oaks are known for living to a ripe old age.

The Art of Shrubs

Topiary is a great way to add a creative touch to your garden. If you fancy giving it a try, all you need is a chicken-wire frame, which should be available ready-made at your local garden centre, and a bit of patience. Once you've decided on a shape, pick a shrub that's roughly the same size (or slightly larger) – box or yew are good varieties for small topiaries – and fit your frame over it and pull the branches through the holes to encourage them to take the shape of the wire. As the shrub slowly grows, simply prune back and trim to create your leafy work of art.

Garden
Structures

Shed Sense

Many people would say that having a shed is one of the best things about a garden – a little bit of man-made order in amongst all that wildness. If you're lucky enough to have space for a shed and are buying one new, look to site it in a sheltered but accessible spot in the garden. It's not usually necessary to obtain planning permission for erecting a shed, but it may be worth consulting your local council office just in case. If you don't have room for a shed, why not put up a screen in the corner of your garden instead?

A garden is the best
alternative therapy.

Germaine Greer

If you're installing a bee hive, a few hemlock plants placed around it will help shelter the bees from cold winds.

Greenhouses

If you have space to take your gardening to the next level with a greenhouse, there are certain things to consider. Perhaps the main point is to judge whether or not you can site your greenhouse in a spot where it will receive uninterrupted sun throughout the day. You should choose a greenhouse with eaves at least 5 feet high, for sufficient light transmission.

Trellises

The most basic use for a trellis is to train climbing plants to grow upwards, creating a delightful vertical display; however they have other uses. If you opt for a trellis with smaller gaps between the slats it can function as a privacy screen and a short trellis can act as a dividing fence. If you're keen to grow sugar or snap peas, cherry tomatoes or cucumbers a trellis is a great way to accommodate such plants.

Garden Lore

Be sure to keep boundary
fences in good order or
you will invite quarrels
with your neighbours.

Furniture

You may think choosing garden furniture is simply a matter of taste, but in fact it pays to think about things like colour in terms of how your furniture will blend with the overall look of your garden – darker shades of paint or plain wood will not detract your eye from the flowers and plants you have in your garden. Space is another key issue – think about purchasing furniture which will give you storage options e.g. a hinged lid seat.

Finishing
Touches

Get the Look

Old-fashioned milk churns, cow bells, cart wheels and farm tools can make interesting outdoor features. Hang them up, lean them against a brick wall or position them in a flower bed to add a touch of traditional rural charm to your garden. If gnomes are your thing, why not try a paint-your-own kit from your local garden centre?

All gardening is
landscape painting.

William Kent

A garden can be a place of sweat and toil, but perhaps the most important thing is to remember to enjoy it!

Chimes

Wind chimes produce a lovey calming sound when caressed by a gentle breeze and will also act to deter birds if necessary. Bamboo chimes produce a softer, more hollow sound than metal ones which ring sweetly – however, both may become irritating if placed in a spot that is too windy, so experiment a little before settling on a final position.

Smart Accessories

Solar-powered lights can be a lovely addition to your borders, especially when you can sit out and enjoy them on lazy summer evenings. A digital garden hose water gauge will help you keep track of your water usage and a pair of plant examining glasses, equipped with special lenses, will allow you to see if your greenery is looking under the weather well before signs appear to the naked eye. And if you fancy getting really hi-tech with your gardening, why not look into one of the many gardening apps available for smart phones and other devices?

Garden Lore

He who plants a garden
plants happiness.

Hanging Around

Presuming you have the space and a suitable tree, a tree swing can really help make the most of your outdoor space and is especially fun for kids! Oak trees are ideal for this – you should select a strong, level branch at least 8 inches in diameter and 10 feet from the ground. Cedar and redwood are both excellent materials for a seat.

Further Reading

BOOKS

General

Greenwood, Pippa *The Gardener's Calendar* (2012, Summersdale)
Jarman, Derek *Derek Jarman's Garden* (1995, Thames and Hudson)
Johnson, Hugh *The Principles of Gardening* (1979, Simon and Schuster)

Planning Your Garden

Alexander, Rosemary *The Essential Garden Design Workbook* (2009, Timber Press)
Crowe, Sylvia *Garden Design* (1999, Garden Art Press)
Young, Chris *RHS Encyclopedia of Garden Design* (2009, Dorling Kindersley)

Soil

Coles, Sarah *Chalk and Limestone Gardening: A Guide to Success on Alkaline Soils* (2005, The Crowood Press Ltd)
Lewis, Wayne; Lowenfels, Jeff *Teaming with Microbes* (2010, Timber Press)
Pitzer, Sara *Gardening in Clay Soil* (1995, Storey Books)

Grass

Darke, Rich *The Encyclopedia of Grasses for Livable Landscapes* (2007, Timber Press)
Hayman, Steven; Sharples, Philip *The Lawn Guide: The Easy Way to a Perfect Lawn* (2008, S&H Publishing)
Hessayon, Dr D G *The Lawn Expert* (1997, Expert)

Greener Gardening

Bowe, Alice High-impact, *Low-carbon Gardening* (2011, Timber Press)
Dominic, Johnnie *Dig That Garden, Save The Planet: Your First Steps to Becoming an Eco-Gardener* (2009, Summersdale)
Green, Charlotte *Gardening Without Water* (1999, Search Press)

Flowers and Plants

Lloyd, Christopher *Garden Flowers* (2001, Weidenfield and Nicolson)
Mabey, Richard *Flora Britannica* (1996, Chatto & Windus/ Sinclair Stevenson)
Brickell, Christopher *The RHS A–Z Encyclopedia of Garden Plants* (2008, Dorling Kindersley)

Growing Fruit, Vegetables and Herbs

Baker, Harry *Growing Fruit* (1999, Mitchell Beazley)
Harrison, John *The Complete Vegetable Grower* (2011, Right Way)
Larkcom, Joy *The Organic Salad Garden* (2003, Frances Lincoln)

Weeding

Flowerdew, Bob *Bob's Basics: Weeding Without Chemicals* (2010, Kyle Cathie)
Hessayon, Dr D G *The Pest and Weed Expert* (2007, Expert)
Thompson, Kenneth *The Book of Weeds* (2009, Dorling Kindersley)

Animals in the Garden

Bardsley, Louise *Wildlife Pond Handbook* (2008, New Holland)
Moss, Stephen *The Garden Bird Handbook* (2011, New Holland Publishers Ltd)
Thomas, Adrian *RSPB Gardening for Wildlife: A Complete Guide to Nature-friendly Gardening* (2010, A&C Black Publishers)

Gardening with Pots

Joyce, David *The Ultimate Container Garden* (2000, Frances Lincoln)
Ott, Steve; Rawlings, Emma; Roxanne, Warwick *Grow Your Own Fruit and Veg in Plot, Pots or Growbags* (2008, Foulsham)
Thomas, Ceri *Gardeners' World: 101 Ideas for Pots* (2007, BBC Books)

Trees

Dunn, Nick *Trees for Your Garden* (2010, Tree Council)
Miller, Diana M. *400 Trees and Shrubs for Small Spaces* (2008, Timber Press)
Titchmarsh, Alan *Alan Titchmarsh How to Garden: Pruning and Training* (2009, BBC Books)

Miscellaneous

Edwards Forkner, Lorene *Handmade Garden Projects* (2012, Timber Press)
Lush, Tony *Garden Buildings Manual* (2007, J H Haynes & co Ltd)
RHS Complete Gardener's Manual (2011, Dorling Kindersley)

General Online Resources

www.bbc.co.uk/learning/subjects/gardening.shtml

www.eatweeds.co.uk

www.kew.org

www.rhs.org.uk/gardening

www.shedman.co.uk

www.telegraph.co.uk/gardening

www.theflowerexpert.com

If you're interested in finding out more about our gift books, follow us on Twitter: @summersdale

www.summersdale.com